ECDL Module 7:
Information and Communication

Springer
London
Berlin
Heidelberg
New York
Barcelona
Hong Kong
Milan
Paris
Singapore
Tokyo

ICDL Approved Courseware
Syllabus Version 3.0

ECDL Approved Courseware
Syllabus Version 3.0

EUROPEAN COMPUTER DRIVING LICENCE and ECDL & STARS Device are trade marks of the European Computer Driving Licence Foundation Limited in Ireland and other countries. Springer Verlag is an independent entity from the European Computer Driving Licence Foundation Limited, and not affiliated with the European Computer Driving Licence Foundation Limited in any manner. This publication may be used in assisting students to prepare for a European Computer Driving Licence Examination. Neither the European Computer Driving Licence Foundation Limited nor Springer Verlag warrants that the use of this publication will ensure the passing the relevant Examination. Use of the ECDL – Approved Courseware logo on this product signifies that it has been independently reviewed and approved in complying with the following standards:

ECDL Module 7: Information and Communication

ECDL – the European PC standard

by **David Stott & Diane Moran**

 Springer

BCS

004.678

394

The Publisher and the BCS would like to publicly acknowledge the vital support of the ECDL Foundation in validating and approving this book for the purpose of studying for the European-wide ECDL qualification.

Springer-Verlag London Ltd, Sweetapple House, Catteshall Road, Godalming, Surrey GU7 3DJ or

The British Computer Society, 1 Sanford Street, Swindon, Wiltshire SN1 1HJ

ISBN 1-85233-448-7

British Library Cataloguing in Publication Data
Stott, David
    ECDL module 7: information and communication: ECDL – the European PC standard. –
    (European computer driving licence)
    1. Electronic mail systems 2. Internet searching
    I. Title II. Moran, Diane
    004.6'78

    ISBN 1852334487

Printed and bound at The Cromwell Press, Trowbridge, Wiltshire, England.
34/3830-543210 Printed on acid-free paper SPIN 10792544

Preface

This book is intended to help you successfully complete the test for Module 7 of the European Computer Driving Licence (ECDL). However before we start working through the actual content of the guide you may find it useful to know a little bit more about the ECDL in general and where this particular Module fits into the overall framework.

What Is The ECDL?

The European Computer Driving Licence (ECDL) is a European-wide qualification that enables people to demonstrate their competence in computer skills. It certifies the candidate's knowledge and competence in personal computer usage at a basic level and is based upon a single agreed syllabus.

This syllabus covers a range of specific knowledge areas and skill sets, which are broken down into seven modules. Each of the modules must be passed before the ECDL certificate can be awarded, though they may be taken in any order but must be completed within a three year period.

Testing of candidates is at audited testing centres, and successful completion of the test will demonstrate the holder's basic knowledge and competence in using a personal computer and common computer applications.

The implementation of the ECDL in the UK is being managed by the British Computer Society. It is growing at a tremendous rate and is set to become the most widely recognised qualification in the field of work-related computer use.

The ECDL Modules

The seven modules which make up the ECDL certificate are described briefly below:

Module 1: Basic Concepts of Information Technology covers the physical make-up of a personal computer and some of the basic concepts of Information Technology such as data storage and memory, and the uses of information networks within computing. It also looks at the application of computer software in society and the use of IT systems in everyday situations. Some basic security and legal issues are also addressed.

Module 2: Using the Computer and Managing Files covers the basic functions of a personal computer and its operating system. In particular it looks at operating effectively within the desktop environment, managing and organising files and directories, and working with desktop icons.

Module 3: Word Processing covers the use of a word processing application on a personal computer. It looks at the basic operations associated with creating, formatting and finishing a word processing document ready for distribution. It also addresses some of the more advanced features such as creating standard tables, using pictures and images within a document, importing objects and using mail merge tools.

Module 4: Spreadsheets covers the basic concepts of spreadsheets and the ability to use a spreadsheet application on a personal computer. Included are the basic operations for developing, formatting and using a spreadsheet, together with the use of basic formulas and functions to carry out standard mathematical and logical operations. Importing objects and creating graphs and charts are also covered.

Module 5: Database covers the basic concepts of databases and the ability to use a database on a personal computer. It addresses the design and planning of a simple database, and the retrieval of information from a database through the use of query, select and sort tools.

Module 6: Presentation covers the use of presentation tools on a personal computer, in particular creating, formatting and preparing presentations. The requirement to create a variety of presentations for different audiences and situations is also addressed.

Module 7: Information and Communication is divided into two main sections, the first of which covers basic Web search tasks using a Web browser and search engine tools. The second section addresses the use of electronic mail software to send and receive messages, to attach documents, and to organise and manage message folders and directories.

This guide focuses upon Module 7.

How To Use This Guide

The purpose of this guide is to take you through all of the knowledge areas and skill sets specified in the syllabus for Module 7. The use of clear, non technical explanations and self paced exercises will provide you with an understanding of the key elements of the syllabus and give you a solid foundation for moving on to take the ECDL test relating to this Module. All exercises contained within this guide are based upon the Windows 98 operating system and Office 97 software.

Each chapter has a well defined set of objectives that relate directly to the syllabus for the ECDL Module 7. Because the guide is structured in a logical sequence you are advised to work through the chapters one at a time from the beginning. Throughout each chapter there are various review questions so that you can determine whether you have understood the principles involved correctly prior to moving on to the next step.

Conventions Used In This Guide

Throughout this guide you will come across notes alongside a number of icons. They are all designed to provide you with specific information related to the section of the book you are currently working through. The icons and the particular types of information they relate to are as follows:

Additional Information: Further information or explanation about a specific point.

Caution: A word of warning about the risks associated with a particular action, together with guidance, where necessary on how to avoid any pitfalls.

Definition: A plain English definition of a newly introduced term or concept.

Short Cuts: Short cuts and hints for using a particular program more effectively.

As you are working through the various exercises contained within this guide, you will be asked to carry out a variety of actions:

- Where we refer to commands or items that you are required to select from the PC screen, then we indicate these in bold, for example: Click on the **Yes** button.
- Where you are asked to key text in to the PC, then we indicate this in italics, for example: Type in the words '*Saving my work*'.

You should now be in a position to use this guide, so lets get started. Good luck!

Contents

Introduction

Module 7 of the ECDL qualification is concerned with the subject of Information and Communication. By this we mean using the Internet as a source of information and a means of electronic communication.

Before embarking on the task of learning how to use the Internet to gather information and to communicate with other computer users it is important that you gain a basic understanding of what the Internet actually is and why it has become a modern day phenomenon.

The Internet: The Internet is a global network of computers which has been developing and evolving since its initial conception in the late 1960's. It has now become a vast collection of more than 88 million interconnected computers with an estimated 300 million users world-wide, growing at a rate of over 100,000 people every day. It is also estimated that there are in excess of 1 billion Web pages currently available online. Therefore it is not surprising that the Internet represents such an important resource for research purposes. In addition, because it operates on a global scale the Internet has proved to be an extremely valuable and fast method of international communication, with an estimated 200 billion individual e-mail messages transmitted annually.

There are two major aspects of using the Internet which are covered in this guide. The first is accessing and using the World Wide Web (WWW), sometimes simply referred to as the Web, in order to view information in the form of Web pages. This is accomplished using what is known as a 'Web Browser', a software program designed to retrieve and display Web pages on your PC.

Using a Web browser you can perform the following tasks:

● Display Web pages on your PC monitor.
● Save Web pages, text based information and graphical information on your PC.
● Search for information located on Web sites.
● Print information retrieved from the Web.
● Mark Web pages so that you can return to them easily.

7

The second major aspect covered by this guide is communicating via the transmission and receipt of electronic messages, simply referred to as Electronic Mail or e-mail for short. E-mail is generated using a software program called a Mail Client which is designed to send and receive e-mail via the Internet.

Using a Mail Client you can perform the following tasks:

● Compose e-mail message to send to other e-mail users.
● Receive messages from other e-mail users.
● Send and receive files.
● Send e-mail message to multiple recipients simultaneously.
● Maintain a list of e-mail addresses.

This guide is structured in chapters that are designed to be followed in a logical sequence, therefore you are advised to work through the guide one chapter at a time from the beginning. At the end of each chapter there are some review questions so that you can check whether you have understood the principles involved correctly.

Getting Started with the Internet

In this chapter you will learn how to

- *Connect your PC to the Internet*
- *Open and close a Web browsing application*
- *Understand the make-up and structure of a Web address*
- *Display a given Web page and, if required, save it as a file*
- *Change the Web browser Home/Start page*
- *Change view/display modes*
- *Modify the toolbar display*
- *Display images on a Web page*

If you already have an Internet connection established on your PC then you can skip this section and proceed straight to 1.1 First Steps with the Internet.

In order to connect to the Internet using your PC you must have three basic things:

1. A telephone line.
2. A modem.
3. An account with an Internet Service Provider (ISP).

Let's look at each one of these items in turn:

The Telephone Line

A telephone line is used to make a dial-up connection to the Internet. Most standard domestic voice telephone lines will allow you to access the Internet. However, if you are in any doubt then speak to the company that provides your telephone service. If you intend to connect to the Internet via an office switchboard then you may need to speak with the switchboard equipment supplier first.

The Modem

A modem is a special piece of equipment which allows your computer to transmit and receive data over a dial-up connection. There are basically two main types of modem; internal and external. An internal modem is a small PC expansion card which is installed inside the computer and has a single cable which plugs directly into a telephone wall socket. External modems are small boxes that are designed to sit on your desk. They require a power connection and have one cable connected to the PC and another cable connected to the telephone wall socket. All modems come with software which is used to install and configure them for use. Nowadays most PCs are supplied with internal modems already fitted as standard but if your PC doesn't have a modem you should talk to your computer supplier before proceeding.

The ISP account

Generally you will need to connect to the Internet via an Internet Service Provider unless the company you work for already has an established Internet connection. An ISP is effectively a gateway to the Internet whereby your computer dials into the ISP computer which is already connected to the Internet itself. However, in order to gain access to the ISP's computer you (the user) must have an existing account which verifies your permission to access it. Due to massive competition in the marketplace there are a large number of ISP's to

choose from, with the majority offering free accounts to users so that
you will generally only have to pay for the cost of telephone calls in
order to access the Internet.

> **If your PC is part of a Local Area Network (LAN) then you
> should talk to the network administrator or supervisor
> about establishing a connection to the Internet.**

First time Internet connection

Assuming that you have a suitable telephone line and modem available
then we can begin to set up an Internet connection. Don't worry if
you don't have an existing account with an ISP as we can register for
an account online during the set up procedure, if necessary.

In order to connect to the Internet for the very first time you need to
use the 'Internet Connection Wizard' which is a standard feature of
Windows 98. Running the Windows 98 Internet Connection Wizard will
setup your computer to use Internet Explorer to browse Web pages,
and Outlook Express to send and receive e-mail. After completing the
steps in the wizard you should just be able to double click on the
Internet Explorer icon on your desktop to connect to the Internet.

The Internet Connection Wizard may appear as an icon on your
desktop like in Figure 1.1 in which case you can simply double click
on it to start it.

**Figure 1.1 Double click here to start the
Internet Connection Wizard.**

> **Wizard: A Wizard within a Microsoft application is a special
> feature which is designed to guide the user step by step
> through a complex process. Generally, when you run a
> wizard you will be presented with a series of dialogue
> boxes that ask you questions. Depending on your answer
> the wizard will configure your system accordingly.**

If there is no icon on your desktop then you can start the Internet Connection Wizard as follows:

Click on the **Start** button and select the **Programs** option. Next, select the **Accessories** menu option followed by the **Internet Tools** option. Here you should see **Internet Connection Wizard** and you should now click on this option, as shown in Figure 1.2.

Figure 1.2 Starting the Internet Connection Wizard from the Start button.

Once started the Internet Connection Wizard will display a dialogue box as shown in Figure 1.3.

Figure 1.3 Using the Internet Connection Wizard to sign up for a new Internet account.

Follow the instructions provided and when you have successfully completed the Internet Connection Wizard process your new Internet connection should be configured and ready for use.

1.1. First Steps with the Internet

Assuming that you have either successfully established an Internet connection with your chosen ISP or that you already had an existing Internet connection then we can now proceed with the task of understanding the first steps of using the Internet.

In this initial section we will look at some basic procedures that will allow us to:

- Open a Web browsing application.
- Understand the make-up and structure of a Web address.
- Display a given Web page.
- Change the Web browser Home Page/Startpage.
- Save a Web page as a file.
- Use application Help functions.
- Close the Web browsing application.

Exercise 1.1

In this exercise we will make use of the Microsoft Internet Explorer version 5 software which is supplied as standard with Windows 98 to look at Web pages.

step **1.** On your Windows desktop there should be an **Internet Explorer** icon as shown in Figure 1.4. Double click on this icon with the left mouse button to start the application. If this icon is not on your desktop then you can start the program by clicking on the **Start** button on the **Task Bar** and selecting **Programs | Internet Explorer**.

Figure 1.4 The Internet Explorer icon on the desktop.

step **2.** After starting Internet Explorer your system will establish a connection to your ISP. Normally this is achieved using a utility called Dial-up Networking (DUN) and depending on how your DUN program has been configured you might see a window like the one shown in Figure 1.5.

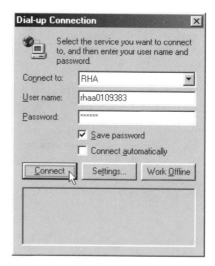

Figure 1.5 The Dial-up Connection window.

 3. Enter the user name and password that were assigned to you when you opened your account with your chosen ISP and click on the **Connect** button to continue. (You can if you wish bypass this stage in the future by ticking the **Save password** and **Connect automatically** check boxes.)

4. Once the connection has been established you will be logged on to the ISP's computer and the Dial-up Connection box will disappear.

> **If you cannot establish a connection with your ISP's computer then you should call their Technical Support Help Desk and they should be able to advise you about how to rectify any connection problems.**

5. Internet Explorer will now display your 'Home' page which is basically your starting point for browsing the World Wide Web (WWW). Normally your 'Home' page will your ISP's default starting page (see Figure 1.6) but as you will see shortly you can change this if you wish.

Figure 1.6 The Internet Explorer main window displaying a typical home page.

6. Internet Web pages are referenced by means of a special address called a Uniform Resource Locator (URL). This is what appears in the Address box when a particular page is being displayed and we can type an address of a specific page for Internet Explorer to find and display. For example, type *http://www.bcs.org.uk* in the **Address** box and press the Return or Enter key on your keyboard, this will take you to the BCS Web site and display the default start page as shown in Figure 1.7.

definition

URL: The World Wide Web (WWW) is a network of electronic files, or Web pages as they are called, stored on numerous computers all around the world. A system known as Hypertext links these resources together. Uniform Resource Locators or URLs are the addresses used to locate these pages and other files on the Internet. The information contained in a URL gives you the ability to jump from one location on the Web to another with just a click of your mouse.

A typical URL will look like the following:

http://www.microsoft.com/

Which in this instance is the start page of Microsoft Corporation in the USA.

A URL is comprised of 2 mandatory parts and 3 optional parts. A URL will always appear in the following order:

Protocol

This can be http, gopher, ftp, mailto, and news. The most common, which every Internet Web site URL begins with, is http (HyperText Transfer Protocol).

Server name

This is the Internet address of the computer or file server where the source (generally a Web page) is stored.

Port Number (optional)

Port numbers rarely appear in a URL because the majority of file servers are located at the Web's default port, which is 80.

Filename (optional)

This is the name the file or Web page has on the server. If the file is in a directory or subdirectory on the server, the path to the file and the name of the file will appear. If no file name is specified then the default file that Web browsers look for and load is index.html.

Anchor(optional)

An anchor is a named bookmark within an HTML (hypertext mark-up language, the language used to "write" Web sites) file.

The following are examples of typical URLs or Web page addresses:

http://www.bbc.co.uk/
http://info.isoc.org/guest/zakon/Internet/History/HIT.html
http://www.altavista.com/
http://msn.co.uk/homepage.asp

Notice that whilst most Web page addresses start with the letters WWW this is not always the case.

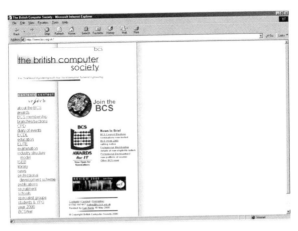

Figure 1.7 The BCS home page displayed in Internet Explorer.

shortcut

When typing in URLs in the Address: box in Internet Explorer you don't have to type in the http:// at the beginning as this is the default. So, if you just type www.microsoft.com then the http:// will be added automatically when you press the Return or Enter key on your keyboard.

step 7. As mentioned previously Internet Explorer uses a 'Home' page which it displays each time the application is started and whilst this is normally the start page of your chosen ISP you can change it if you wish. There are two ways to specify a new home page in Internet Explorer. Make sure that the page you want to use as your new home page is already displayed in Internet Explorer and then select **Tools I Internet Options...** on the Menu Bar, a tabbed dialogue box like the one shown in Figure 1.8 will be displayed. Here you can simply click on the **Use Current** button and then the **Apply** or **OK** buttons to set your new home page. Alternatively you can type in an address of a Web page to use as your home page in the **Address:** box and then click on the Apply or OK buttons. The next time you start Internet Explorer it will display your new home page as your starting point for Web browsing.

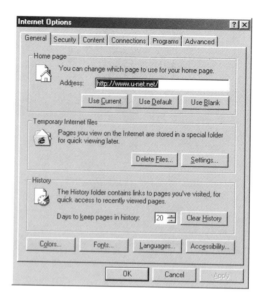

Figure 1.8 Setting a new home page.

The Internet is extremely dynamic in nature and things are changing all the time. Web pages in particular are being constantly updated, modified and replaced and therefore you cannot always expect a particular page to appear exactly the same each time you visit a site. Don't be surprised if any of the examples used in this guide look completely different when you open them in Internet Explorer.

8. In order to access and view a Web page you must be online to the Internet so that the information can be retrieved from the appropriate Web server. However, it is also possible to view Web pages that are stored locally on your own PC. Therefore Internet Explorer gives you the option of saving a Web page so that you can view it when you are offline. This can be very useful if you wish to keep a particular Web page for future reference or if you wish to avoid paying for the telephone call in order to read a long detailed page of information. Let's start by going to the ECDL home page at http://www.ecdl.com, so type this URL in the **Address** box and press the Return or Enter key. Once the page is displayed select **File | Save As...** from the Menu Bar and a dialogue box as shown in Figure 1.9 will be displayed.

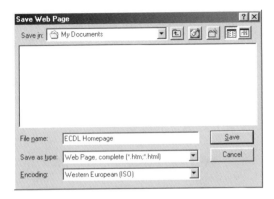

Figure 1.9 The Save As dialogue box.

9. By default Internet Explorer uses the **My Documents** folder to store any Web pages that you save but you can if you wish select a different folder using the **Save in:** drop down list. Internet Explorer also uses the actual Web page name as the file name for the saved page and you can change this if you wish. To save the page click on the **Save** button and the **Save Web Page** window will disappear.

10. To open a Web page that you have previously saved select **File I Open...** from the Menu Bar and a dialogue box as shown in Figure 1.10 will appear.

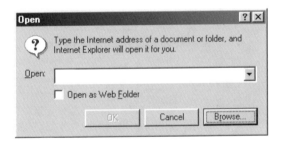

Figure 1.10 The File Open dialogue box.

11. Here you should click on the **Browse** button and then select the **My Documents** folder and click on the **Open** button. Select the file that you want to open, as in Figure 1.11, and then click on the **Open** button again. The Web page will then be displayed in Internet Explorer.

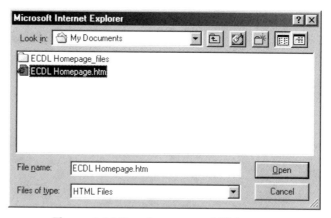

Figure 1.11 Opening a saved Web page.

step **12.** If you get stuck when using Internet Explorer and you don't know how to perform a particular task then there is an in-built Help system where you might find an answer to your problem. You can access Help at any time by pressing the F1 key on your keyboard or clicking on the **Help I Contents and Index** option on the Menu Bar. This displays a window with 3 tabbed sections **Contents**, **Index** and **Search**. In addition, there is an easy to use Web page type interface on the right hand side with hypertext links to other help pages as shown in Figure 1.12.

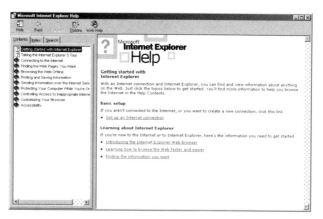

Figure 1.12 The Internet Explorer Help system.

step **13.** Clicking on the **Contents** tab presents you with a list of Help contents for you to select from. Note that the main contents sections may have sub-sections, as in Figure 1.13.

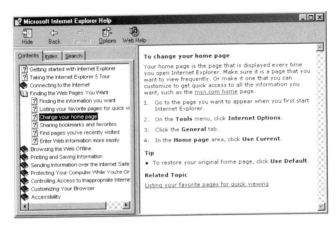

Figure 1.13 The Help Topics Contents tab showing sub sections.

step 14. Selecting the **Index** tab displays a list of indexed keywords that are available in the help system. You simply click on the index word you want and then click on the **Display** button as in Figure 1.14.

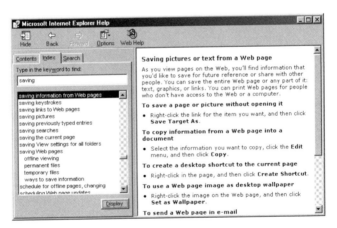

Figure 1.14 You can search for keywords in the Index section.

step 15. Clicking on the **Search** tab allows you to look for any word or phrase and the Help system will then show you any matches that it can find. Type a word or phrase, such as URL, in the box provided and then click on the **List Topics** button. Once again you can simply select any found topic and click on the **Display** button to see it, as in Figure 1.15.

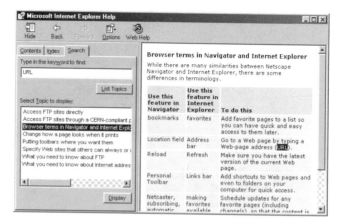

Figure 1.15 The Search section lets you look for any words or phrases.

16. Finally in this section you can close Internet Explorer by selecting the **File | Close** option on the Menu Bar. If you are connected to your ISP when you close Internet Explorer you may see an **Auto Disconnect** dialogue box displayed asking you whether you want to stay connected or not as in the example shown in Figure 1.16. Normally you should click on the **Disconnect Now** button to terminate your telephone call but you can if you wish click on **Stay Connected** so that if you start Internet Explorer again you don't have to wait for a connection to be established before continuing to view other online Web pages.

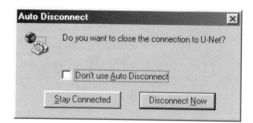

Figure 1.16 The Auto Disconnect dialogue box.

Summary

In this first section we have seen how to start Internet Explorer and display Web pages by typing in URLs in the address box. You should now be aware of the make-up and structure of Web addresses and how to display a given Web page. We have also seen how Internet Explorer uses a Home page when it starts and how you can change this to any Web page you like.

Web pages can be saved on your local PC and then viewed offline if you wish. If you get stuck you can access the Internet Explorer Help system in order to solve problems.

Finally, we have seen that when you close Internet Explorer you will be given the option of disconnecting from your ISP.

1.2. Adjust Basic Settings

Now that we have seen how to start Internet Explorer, view Web pages and use the Help system it is time to look at some of the basic settings that we can use to control and manage the application.

In this section you will learn how to:

● Change view/display modes.
● Modify the toolbar display.
● Display images on a Web page.
● Prevent the loading of image files onto Web pages.

Exercise 1.2

1. If it is not already open, you should start Internet Explorer by either double clicking the icon on the desktop or by clicking on the **Start** button on the **Task Bar** and selecting **Programs | Internet Explorer**. Once started, your current home page will be displayed.

2. We can change the way pages are displayed within Internet Explorer in several ways. For example, select **View | Text Size** on the Menu Bar and a small pop-up menu appears with 5 options on it as shown in Figure 1.17. By default the text size is set to **Medium** as evident by the black dot next to the option. However, you can select any of the 5 options and the text on the current Web page and any subsequent Web pages that you view will be adjusted accordingly until the **Text Size** is altered again.

Figure 1.17 Adjusting the text size.

step **3.** As well as adjusting the size of text displayed we can view a Web page full screen by selecting the **View I Full Screen** option on the Menu Bar. Choosing this option removes the window Title Bar, the Address Bar and the Menu Bar from the top of the screen, along with the Status Bar from the bottom of the screen. In addition the Standard Toolbar is replaced with a smaller version which takes up less space so that more of the Web page can be seen, as shown in Figure 1.18. To return to the normal Web page view click on the **Restore** button window control.

Figure 1.18 A Web page viewed Full Screen.

shortcut

You can quickly switch between the Normal and Full Screen views of a Web page by pressing the F11 key on your keyboard.

step **4.** We have briefly mentioned Toolbars in passing and using the **View I Toolbars** option on the Menu Bar we can turn the display of the Standard Toolbar and the Address Toolbar on and off. In addition, there are two further toolbars; Links (which are predefined Web page addresses) and Radio (which can be used to control radio broadcasts over the Internet). Each of these toolbars can also be turned on or off using the **View I Toolbars** option as shown in Figure 1.19.

Figure 1.19 All 4 Internet Explorer toolbars displayed.

5. Most Web pages consist of a mixture of text and graphics. However, text downloads and displays itself far quicker than graphics and there may be occasions when you wish to view a Web page without displaying the graphics. Fortunately you can do this in Internet Explorer by selecting the **Tools | Internet Options...** on the Menu Bar and then displaying the **Advanced** tab as shown in Figure 1.20. Here under the **Multimedia** section there is an option labelled **Show pictures** and if you deselect this check box then when you view a Web page the graphics will not be displayed as indicated in Figure 1.21.

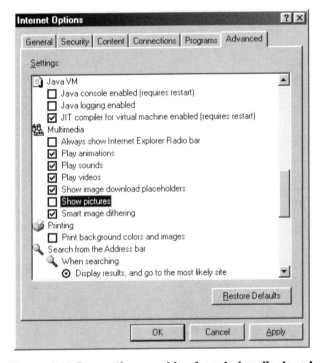

Figure 1.20 Preventing graphics from being displayed.

Download: The term download or downloading refers to the process of data transfer from a host computer such as a Web server to a client computer such as your PC. The opposite is of course upload or uploading whereby you are sending data from your PC to the host system.

Figure 1.21 The BCS Web page without graphics.

6. Notice when you turn off the option to **Show pictures** the graphics themselves are no longer displayed but the boxes which hold the images are still visible as in Figure 1.21. If you want to remove these image placeholders as they are called, you should re-select the **Show pictures** check box and deselect the **Show image download placeholders** instead as shown in Figure 1.22. This then removes all the image boxes from the page leaving just the text as in Figure 1.23.

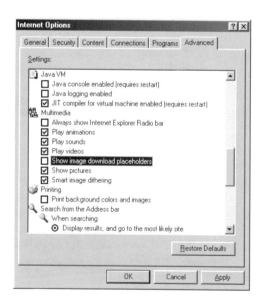

Figure 1.22 Removing the image placeholders.

Figure 1.23 The BCS page without placeholders.

Certain pictures on Web pages contain hypertext links to other Web pages so that you can click on them to display more information. If you turn off the displaying of graphics then these hypertext links will still be there on the page and you can still use them in the same way. The only difference is you will not be able to easily see whereabouts on the page the links are without the graphics to guide you.

Summary

Internet Explorer provides several options for controlling how a Web page is displayed. For example, we can increase or decrease the size of the text, prevent graphics from being displayed, and even stop the image placeholders from appearing on a Web page.

In addition, we have seen how we can display the various toolbars available in Internet Explorer and view a Web page in Full Screen mode so that we can see more of it than in the Normal view.

Review Questions

1. What are the 3 basic requirements for connecting to the Internet?

2. What function does a modem perform?

3. What is the basic procedure for starting Internet Explorer from the Windows desktop?

4. What is a Wizard?

5. What is a 'Home' page?

6. How many mandatory parts does a URL have?

7. Describe the procedure for changing your home page.

8. Which Menu Bar option would you use to view a saved Web page?

9. Which keyboard key should you press to invoke the online Help in Internet Explorer?

10. How do you close Internet Explorer?

11. How many different text sizes are available for viewing Web pages?

12. Which keyboard key would you use to switch between Normal and Full Screen views of a Web page?

13. How can you prevent graphics from displaying on Web pages?

14. What is meant by the term download?

2

Web Navigation

In this chapter you will learn how to

- *Open a URL (Uniform Resource Locator)*
- *Navigate through the WWW using hypertext links*
- *Browse a specified site and collect data*
- *Download files from the WWW*

Now that we have covered some of the basic principles of connecting to the Internet and viewing Web pages with Internet Explorer we need to look at the various ways in which we can navigate around the WWW.

2.1. Accessing a Web Address

In this chapter we will look at accessing Web addresses in more detail and you will learn how to perform the following tasks:

● Open a URL (Uniform Resource Locator) and collect data.
● Open a hypertext link or image link and return to the original page.
● Browse a specified site and collect data.

Exercise 2.1

step **1.** Once again, if it is not already open you should start Internet Explorer by either double clicking the icon on the desktop or by clicking on the **Start** button on the **Task Bar** and selecting **Programs I Internet Explorer**. As soon as you have established an Internet connection and your current home page is displayed we are ready to proceed.

step **2.** As mentioned previously most Web pages contain hypertext links or hyperlinks which you can click on to display further information. A hypertext link can take you to a different part of the same page (especially if it is a long one), a new page on the same Web site, or even a page on a completely different Web site (usually related in some way). For example, go to the BCS main page again by typing the address www.bcs.org.uk in the **Address** box and pressing the Return or Enter key on your keyboard. Notice how some of the text on this page is displayed in blue and underlined. These are the hypertext links and clicking on them will take you to different Web pages. As you move the mouse pointer over these hypertext links the pointer changes from an arrow to a 'pointing finger' symbol to indicate that this is a link that you can click on to go somewhere else. On the BCS main Web page click on the link called **branches/sections** as shown in Figure 2.1.

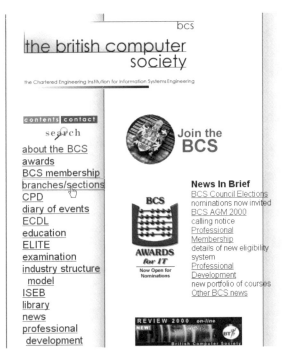

Figure 2.1 Clicking on a hypertext link to view another Web page.

3. Next, scroll down the BCS Branches Directory page until you see the reference to **Manchester** and click on this hypertext link as shown in Figure 2.2.

Figure 2.2 Selecting a hypertext link.

step **4.** When the new Web page is displayed you will notice in the Address Bar that we have been taken to a completely different Web site at http://www.ksap.demon.co.uk/bcs/ as shown in Figure 2.3.

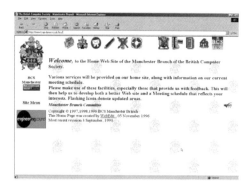

Figure 2.3 The www.ksap.demon.co.uk/bcs/ Web page.

step **5.** To return to the previous Web page click on the **Back** button on the Toolbar. Once you have viewed a number of Web pages you can use the **Back** and **Forward** buttons to step through the Web pages that Internet Explorer has previously displayed.

step **6.** We have already seen how we can save Web pages for viewing when offline but there are other ways that we can collect data from the WWW. Certain Web pages offer the option of downloading information in the form of files. This uses a special Internet feature called the File Transfer Protocol (FTP) to transfer data from a Web site and enable you to save a file directly to your PC's hard disk. For example, enter www.scottishgift.com/wallpaper.htm in the **Address Bar** in Internet Explorer and you should see the page illustrated in Figure 2.4 displayed.

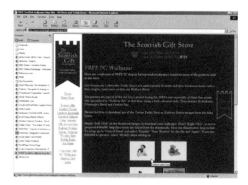

Figure 2.4 Downloading an image file.

7. Now if you click on one of the images displayed on the page you will see a dialogue box as shown in Figure 2.5. Select the **Save this file to disk** option and click on the **OK** button. The **Save As** dialogue box will now appear for you to specify a location and file name for the file you wish to save, as shown in Figure 2.6.

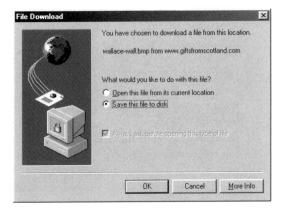

Figure 2.5 Saving a download file to disk.

Figure 2.6 Specifying a location for saving a file download.

8. When you click on the **Save** button the file will be transferred from the host Web site and be saved on your local PC hard disk. Once the file has been successfully downloaded you can access it even when you are not online to the Internet. Note that the example we have downloaded is a Windows .bmp file which you can open using the Windows Paint program.

caution!

When downloading files from Web sites there are 3 things of which you need to be aware:

Copyright – Certain information whether it is text, graphics, audio or video available on the Internet is subject to copyright. Therefore, before you download anything, you should check whether an item is copyright protected.

Large files – Many image, audio and video files are extremely large and consequently they can take a long time to download (especially if your connection to the Internet is slow). Downloading large files can be an expensive procedure but fortunately you can cancel the operation at any time.

Viruses – Any file which contains executable code, such as a program or a document with macros in it could contain a virus which may damage or delete any data stored on your hard disk. Therefore you should use appropriate Anti-Virus software to check any files that you download from a Web site before running them.

9. There is another way in which you can collect data from a Web page even if there is no option displayed to download it. For example, enter metalab.unc.edu/wm/paint/auth/vinci/joconde/joconde.jpg in the **Address Bar** and press the Return or Enter key on your keyboard. You should now see a picture of the Mona Lisa as shown in Figure 2.7. However there is no option on this Web page to download the image file. However, if you select the **File I Save As...** option on the Menu Bar the **Save Picture** dialogue box that appears allows you to save the image as a file, as shown in Figure 2.8.

Figure 2.7 The Mona Lisa displayed on a Web page.

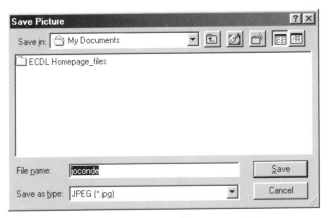

Figure 2.8 Saving a picture as a file.

shortcut

As well as using the File I Save As... option on the Menu Bar you can save an image displayed on a Web page using the mouse. Point to the image you want to save and press the right hand mouse button. A short cut menu will appear and you can then select the Save Picture As... option.

Summary

In this section we have seen how it is possible to navigate through the WWW using hypertext links as well as the **Back** and **Forward** buttons on the Toolbar. We have also looked at the different ways that files can be downloaded and how an image can be saved as a file on your PC's hard disk.

Review Questions

1. What is a hypertext link or a hyperlink?

2. How can you recognise hyperlinks on a Web page using the mouse?

3. Which two buttons on the Toolbar let you navigate through Web pages that you have already viewed?

4. What is the Internet feature that enables you to download files called?

5. What are the 3 things you need to be aware of when downloading files from the Internet?

6. If there is no download option on a Web page how can you save an image to your local hard disk?

Web Searching

In this chapter you will learn how to

- *Define search requirements when using a search engine*

- *Use keywords and common logical operators when undertaking a search*

- *Print a Web page using the basic print options*

- *Adjust the setup options for printing, where appropriate*

- *Present a search report as a printed document*

With in excess of 600 million Web pages the WWW is huge and growing all the time. As a result it can often be very difficult to pinpoint specific information. Fortunately the WWW itself comes to the rescue, as there are facilities widely available that you can use to search for information on the Internet.

3.1. Using a Search Engine

Search Engines are just like other Web pages but they allow you to enter search terms in text form, which the system will then search for and display the results on a new Web page.

In this section you will learn how to:

● Define search requirements.
● Use a keyword in a search.
● Use common logical operators in a search.

Exercise 3.1

step **1.** For this exercise we will use a Search Engine called All the Web. So, if it is not already loaded, start Internet Explorer by either double clicking the icon on the desktop or by clicking on the **Start** button on the **Task Bar** and selecting **Programs I Internet Explorer**. Next, type *http://www.ussc.alltheweb.com/* into the **Address Bar** and press the Return or Enter key on your keyboard. You should now see a Web page similar to the one shown in Figure 3.1.

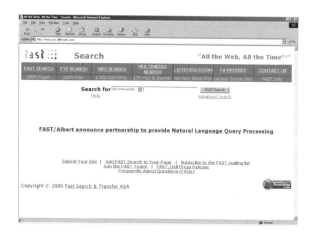

Figure 3.1 All the Web search engine main page.

2. We are going to use the All the Web search engine to look for information about collecting postage stamps and in particular the Penny Black stamp featuring the head of Queen Victoria. Let's start by entering the word '*stamps*' in the **Search for** box and clicking on the **FAST Search** button. A new page is displayed showing the results of the search and in our example over 800,000 Web pages have been found containing the word 'stamps' as shown in Figure 3.2.

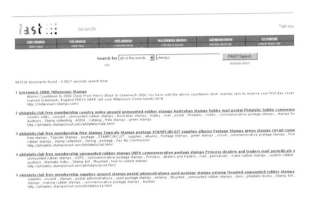

Figure 3.2 Initial search on stamps.

3. This is obviously far too many Web pages to look at in detail and therefore we need to narrow our search down a little. So, let's add the words '*Penny Black*' after '*stamps*' in the **Search for** box and click on the **FAST Search** button again. This time the results displayed have been reduced to a little over 8,000, as shown in Figure 3.3. Whilst this is better it is still too many to look at in detail.

Figure 3.3 Narrowing down our search.

4. We can refine our search even further by adding more words. However, this time we will add the words *"Queen Victoria"* using double quotes which tells the search engine to look for the exact two words in combination rather than the word Queen and the word Victoria separately. This time our results are even smaller with just 420 Web pages found as shown in Figure 3.4. You can now click on any of the hyperlinks listed and that specific page will be displayed. Use the **Back** button on the toolbar to return to the search results page.

Figure 3.4 Refining our search.

step **5.** Each time we extra add words to our search or when we enclose words in double quotes we reduce the number of Web pages that the search engine finds. We can also exclude specific words from our search to reduce the number of results. For example, enter the words '*The Planets Suite*' in the **Search for** box and click on the **FAST Search** button. As you might expect nearly every one of the 300 odd results contains a reference to the composer Holst, as shown in Figure 3.5.

Figure 3.5 Search for "The Planets Suite".

6. However, if we exclude the word Holst by changing the **Search for** box to read '*The Planets Suite-Holst*' the number of Web pages found is dramatically reduced to less than 30, as shown in Figure 3.6. This is an example of using a logical operator in a search engine and different Internet search engines use different techniques to achieve the same sort of results. Generally, on each search engine Web site there will be a hypertext link to a Help page which will give you specific instructions on how to use the system effectively.

Figure 3.6 Using a logical operator to reduce search results.

There are many different search engines available on the WWW and each offers its own particular features and benefits. Some of the most popular ones are listed here for you to try out.

http://www.altavista.com/
http://www.askjeeves.com/
http://www.excite.com/
http://www.alltheweb.com/
http://www.go.com/
http://www.google.com/
http://www.hotbot.com/
http://www.inktomi.com/
http://www.lycos.com/
http://search.msn.com/
http://search.netscape.com/
http://www.webcrawler.com/
http://www.yahoo.com/

Summary

We have seen how we can use search engines to help us find specific information on the Internet. By including more words and using double quotes around words and phrases we can reduce the results of a search in order to home in on whatever specific item we are looking for. In addition, we have seen how we can use logical operators to refine our searches so that they are more accurate.

As with most things to do with the WWW you should explore the Internet and experiment with different search engines to see which ones best suit your needs.

3.2. Printing

Whilst most users of the Internet tend to view information solely on the screen there may be occasions when you might want to print some information.

In this section you will learn how to:

- ● Modify page setup options.
- ● Print a Web page using basic print options.
- ● Present a search report as a printed document.

Exercise 3.2

1. Once again, if it is not already open you should start Internet Explorer by either double clicking the icon on the desktop or by clicking on the **Start** button on the **Task Bar** and selecting **Programs I Internet Explorer**. As soon as you have established an Internet connection and your current home page is displayed we are ready to proceed.

2. Any Web page that is currently being displayed in Internet Explorer can be printed. However, before you print you may need to adjust the setup options for the page. To do this select **File I Page Setup...** from the Menu Bar and a dialogue box like the one shown in Figure 3.7 will be displayed.

Figure 3.7 The Page Setup dialogue box.

3. Here you can specify the **Paper Size** you intend to use; define any **Headers** or **Footers** to be printed on each page; select either **Portrait** or **Landscape** mode for the printed pages; and adjust the page **Margins**. You can also select a specific **Printer...** to use. Once you are satisfied with your chosen page settings click on the **OK** button to close the dialogue box.

4. To print a Web page simply select **File I Print...** on the Menu Bar and the **Print** dialogue box will be displayed as shown in Figure 3.8. Here you can select the **Print Range** and specify the number of **Copies** you want to print. Click on the **OK** button to start the print process.

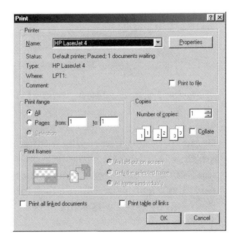

Figure 3.8 Controlling the printing process.

shortcut

Instead of using the File | Print... option from the Menu Bar you can simply click on the Print   icon on the Toolbar. However if you do this then you forego the opportunity of changing any Print settings and the print will be produced using the default settings, which are: the current default Windows printer, print All pages, and print 1 Copy of the current Web page.

5. Occasionally you might wish to print a specific area of a Web page such as the results from a search engine. You can do this by selecting an area on the currently displayed Web page by clicking with the left mouse button and dragging the pointer across this area, which turns blue as you select it as shown in Figure 3.9. Next, if you select **File | Print...** from the Menu Bar and click on the **Selection** option in the **Print Range** area, then only the area selected on your Web page will be printed.

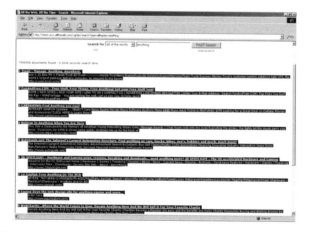

Figure 3.9 Selecting an area of a Web page for printing.

caution!

Because they are primarily intended to be displayed on a monitor many Web pages make extensive use of colour graphics and patterned backgrounds. Therefore you may find that if you print them out using a monochrome printer they can be quite difficult to read.

Summary

In this section we have seen that it is relatively easy to print any Web page that is currently displayed in Internet Explorer. In addition, you can control the Page Setup and the Print process by using the options on the Menu Bar. If necessary you can also select specific areas of a Web page to be printed.

Review Questions

1. What is a Search Engine?

2. How can you reduce the number of results that a Search Engine generates?

3. If you need to search for an exact phrase how would you enter it?

4. How can you exclude specific words from your search?

5. If you are using a particular Search Engine for the first time how can you get help on using its facilities?

6. Which Menu Bar option would you use to control the layout of a printed page?

7. How can you instruct Internet Explorer to print on a particular printer?

8. You need to print just a portion of a Web page. How can you do this?

9. You need 10 copies of a Web page but you don't have access to a photocopier. How can you easily produce these?

4

Bookmarks

In this chapter you will learn how to

- *Create and use bookmarks*
- *Organise and manage bookmarks*

As we have seen previously you can type a URL in the Address box in Internet Explorer and provided that the page is currently available it will be displayed on your screen. However, Web page addresses can be long and complicated and it is very easy to make a mistake whilst typing an address. Fortunately, Internet Explorer has a feature known as Favorites which allows you to 'bookmark' a page so that you can visit it again easily.

In this section you will learn how to:

● Create and use bookmarks
● Organise and manage bookmarks

4.1. Create a Bookmark

The Favorites option in Internet Explorer enables us to: bookmark a Web page, open a bookmarked Web page, and add Web pages to a bookmark folder.

Exercise 4.1

Bookmarks or Favorites are extremely easy to create and any Web page can be bookmarked for future reference.

1. To create a Favorite you need to have the actual page that you want bookmarked displayed in Internet Explorer. Go to the page by either typing the URL in the **Address** box and pressing the Return or Enter key on the keyboard, or click on a hypertext link from another Web page.

2. Once the page you want to bookmark is displayed select **Favorites I Add to Favorites...** option on the Menu Bar. A small dialogue box will appear as shown in Figure 4.1.

Figure 4.1 Adding a specific Web page to your list of Favorites.

3. The **Name** box will automatically be filled in based on the page's title. However, you can overtype this suggestion with anything that you like.

step **4.** Click on the **OK** button and the bookmark will be saved in your Favorites list.

step **5.** To open a bookmarked page click on the **Favorites** menu option and a drop down list of your current Favorites will appear as shown in Figure 4.2. Simply select the one you want and Internet Explorer will take you to that page automatically.

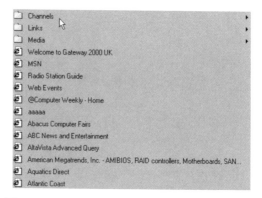

Figure 4.2 Selecting a bookmarked Favorite.

step **6.** When you create a new bookmark it will be placed in the main Favorites folder by default. However, you can if you wish store a bookmark in a sub-folder which you have created. Using sub-folders can help you keep related bookmarks together and organised. With the **Add Favorite** dialogue box open click on the **Create In >>** button and a list of existing sub-folders will appear, as shown in Figure 4.3. Select the target sub folder and click on OK.

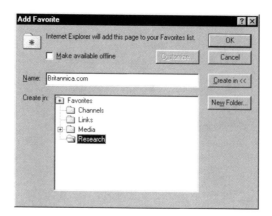

Figure 4.3 Storing a Favorite in a specific folder.

step **7.** If you want to create a new sub-folder to place your bookmark in, then click

on the **New Folder...** button and the **Create New Folder** dialogue box will appear, as shown in Figure 4.4. Type the name of the new folder and click **OK**.

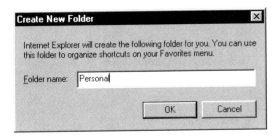

Figure 4.4 Creating a new folder.

8. Note that any new folders will be created in relation to where in the folder hierarchy (tree structure) you actually start from. In this example the folder **Personal** appears as a sub-folder of **Research**, as in the example shown in Figure 4.5.

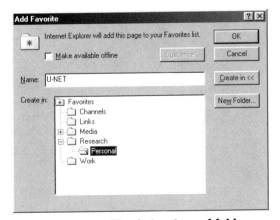

Figure 4.5 The 'Tree' structure of folders.

Summary

In this section we have covered the various procedures required to create and use bookmarks or Favorites. As we have seen the ability to create bookmarks is extremely useful if you intend to return to a particular Web page sometime in the future – you don't have to remember the actual URL which can be quite long and complicated. We have also seen how to create sub-folders to store our Favorites in so that they can be more easily arranged.

4.2. Organising Bookmarks

Over a period of time people generally amass quite large numbers of bookmarks and as a result they may need to rearrange these and organise them in different folders. In this instance the Organize Favorites feature in Internet Explorer can be used to:

- Create a folder
- Rename a folder or bookmark
- Move a bookmark to a folder
- Delete a folder or bookmark

Exercise 4.2

Using the Organize Favorites feature to manage your bookmarks.

1. Click on the **Favorites I Organize Favorites...** on the menu options and the following dialogue box will appear, as shown in Figure 4.6.

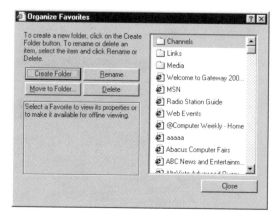

Figure 4.6 Using the Organize Favorites feature.

2. This box displays a scrolling list of all your current bookmarks and folders and has 4 option buttons – **Create Folder, Rename, Move to Folder**, and **Delete**. We will deal with each one in turn. Click on the **Create Folder** button and you will notice that unlike the **New Folder** option in the **Add Favorite** options this button forces you to create a folder at the end of the list of existing folders, as shown in Figure 4.7.

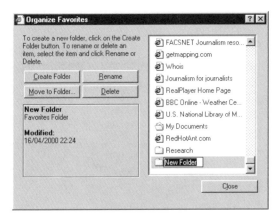

Figure 4.7 Creating a New Folder.

3. Type the name of the new folder and press the Return or Enter on the keyboard to accept it.

You cannot create a sub folder within another folder with the Create Folder option button in the Organize Favorites dialogue box.

4. Next select an entry (either a bookmark or a folder) in the scrolling list on the right and click on the **Rename** button. You can now change the original name of the item to something else, as shown in Figure 4.8.

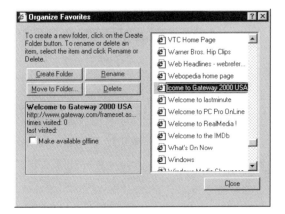

Figure 4.8 Using the Rename option.

5. Select another entry in the scrolling list and click on the **Move to Folder...**

button. A new dialogue box called **Browse for Folder** is displayed, as shown in Figure 4.9.

Figure 4.9 Moving items using the Browse for Folder dialogue box.

step **6.** From here you can select the target folder where the item selected in the scrollable list will be placed. Once the target folder is selected click on **OK** and the **Browse for Folder** dialogue will disappear and you will see the **Organize Favorites** box again with the item we selected in its new location.

step **7.** Finally, select an item in the scrolling list and click on the **Delete** button. You will then be asked to **Confirm Folder** (or **File**) **Delete**, as shown in Figure 4.10.

Figure 4.10 Confirming a deletion.

Summary

Obviously the more bookmarks that you have the more likely you are to need to organise them properly. As a result you should find the Organize Favorites facilities provided by Internet Explorer very useful.

Review Questions

1. What is a bookmark?

2. How do you display a bookmarked Web page?

3. What procedure would you use to create a new folder for storing your Favorites in?

4. How can you move a Favorite to another folder?

Getting Started with Electronic Mail

In this chapter you will learn how to

- *Open and close an electronic mail application*
- *Open a mail inbox for a specified user*
- *Open a mail message*
- *Change display modes for Outlook Express*
- *Modify the toolbar display when using Outlook Express*

Now that we have covered the essential elements of using Internet Explorer to access the WWW it's time to look at a completely different aspect of using the Internet, namely Electronic Mail or e-mail as it is generally known.

definition

e-mail: Essentially e-mail is a mechanism for sending text messages from one computer user to another. This was one of the first real business applications used extensively on the Internet. Even today e-mail is still the most widely used application on the Internet. A basic e-mail message consists of the recipient's address, an optional subject line, and a message body containing lines of text.

5.1. First Steps with Electronic Mail

For this part of the guide we will be using Microsoft Outlook Express version 5 which is supplied as standard with Windows 98.

In this section you will learn how to:

● Open an electronic mail application.
● Open a mail inbox for a specified user.
● Open a mail message.
● Use application Help functions.
● Close the electronic mail application.

Exercise 5.1

step **1.** On your Windows desktop there should be an **Outlook Express** icon as shown in Figure 5.1. Double click on this icon with the left mouse button to start the application. If this icon is not on your desktop then you can start the program by clicking on the **Start** button on the **Task Bar** and selecting **Programs I Outlook Express**.

Figure 5.1 The Outlook Express icon on the desktop.

step **2.** When you start Outlook Express for the very first time you will see a window similar to the example shown in Figure 5.2. Note that if there are no mail accounts already in existence you must run the wizard to **Set up a Mail account...** before proceeding any further. This wizard will guide you through the process step by step but you will need the information relating to mail server addresses provided by your ISP when you opened your e-mail account.

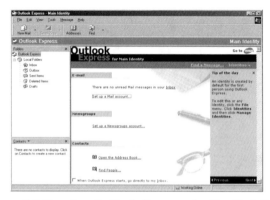

Figure 5.2 Running Outlook Express for the first time.

step **3.** After setting up your mail account you should click on the word **Inbox** which is listed in the **Folders** section of the main window. Your screen should now look similar to the example shown in Figure 5.3. At the top is a list of e-mail messages that have been received in the order in which they arrived. Next to each e-mail message is a small icon which indicates mail which has been read, or indicates any unread mail. To read an e-mail message simply click on the message header which appears in the top window and the body of the message will be displayed in the bottom window. The envelope icons change automatically as you read each mail message. To the right of the envelope icon is the sender's name or e-mail address followed by the subject line and the timestamp detailing when the message was received.

Figure 5.3 Viewing the contents of the Inbox.

step **4.** You can access the Outlook Express online help system at any time by pressing the F1 key on your keyboard or clicking on the **Help | Contents and Index** option on the Menu Bar. This displays a window with 3 tabbed sections **Contents**, **Index** and **Search**. In addition, there is an easy to use Web page-type interface on the right hand side with hypertext links to other help pages as shown in Figure 5.4.

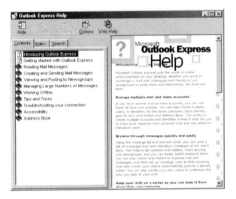

Figure 5.4 Accessing Help in Outlook Express.

step **5.** Clicking on the **Contents** tab presents you with a list of Help contents for you to select from. Note that the main contents sections may have sub-sections, as in Figure 5.5.

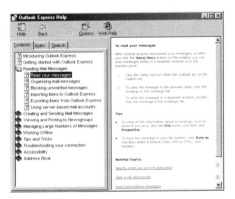

Figure 5.5 Using the Help Contents to display a help topic.

step **6.** Selecting the **Index** tab displays a list of indexed keywords that are available in the help system. You simply click on the index word you want and then click on the **Display** button as in Figure 5.6.

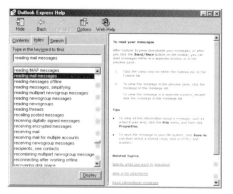

Figure 5.6 The Index tab lists all the indexed keywords in the Help system.

7. Clicking on the **Search** tab allows you to look for any word or phrase and the Help system will then show you all of the matches that it can find. Type a word or phrase in the box provided and then click on the **List Topics** button. Once again you can simply select any topic that has been found and click on the **Display** button to see it, as in Figure 5.7.

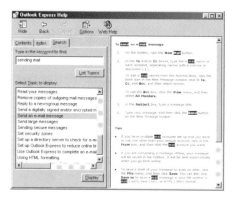

Figure 5.7 The Search tab allows you to look for relevant help.

8. Finally in this section you can close Outlook Express by selecting the **File | Close** option on the Menu Bar. If you are connected to your ISP when you close Outlook Express you may see an **Auto Disconnect** dialogue box displayed asking you whether you want to stay connected or not as in the example shown in Figure 5.8. Normally you should click on the **Disconnect Now** button to terminate your telephone call.

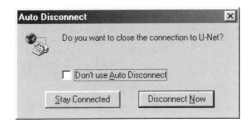

Figure 5.8 The Auto Disconnect dialogue box.

Summary

In this section we have seen how to start Outlook Express and setup a mail account for use. We have also looked at the Inbox and how to open and read any e-mail messages that have been received. If you get stuck you can use the Help system to find a possible solution to your problem.

5.2. Adjust Basic Settings

Now that we have seen how to start Outlook Express and view e-mail messages it is time to look at some of the basic settings that we can use to control and manage the application.

In this section we will see how to:

● Change display modes.
● Modify the toolbar display.

Exercise 5.2

1. If it is not already open you should start Outlook Express by either double clicking the icon on the desktop or by clicking on the **Start** button on the **Task Bar** and selecting **Programs I Outlook Express**. After the application has started, click on the **Inbox** folder in the **Folders** list to display its contents.

2. We can change the appearance of Outlook Express by selecting **View I Layout...** from the Menu Bar. This displays a **Window Layout Properties** dialogue box as shown in Figure 5.9.

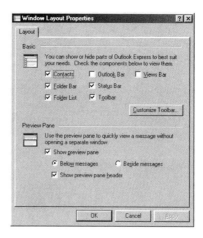

Figure 5.9 Changing the appearance of Outlook Express.

3. This window is split into two sections with the **Basic** settings at the top and the **Preview Pane** settings at the bottom. Let's start by hiding all the various parts of Outlook Express by un-checking all the tick boxes in the **Basic** section. After doing this you should click on the **Apply** button followed by the **OK** button and your Outlook Express window should look something like the example shown in Figure 5.10. Notice how we have removed all the components leaving just the e-mail message headers at the top with the message preview window at the bottom.

Figure 5.10 The most basic Layout with just the e-mail headers and the Preview Pane.

4. Next, let's reverse the process and display all the basic components to see what happens. To do this select **View I Layout...** from the Menu Bar again and check all the tick boxes in the **Basic** section and click on the **Apply**

button followed by the **OK** button. Now as shown in Figure 5.11 there are lots of different window sub-sections displayed. You can decide which of these is most suitable for your particular way of working and then hide any components that you don't need displayed.

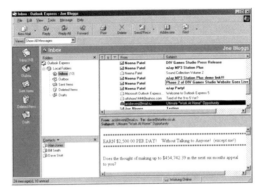

Figure 5.11 Using the Layout options to display all components in Outlook Express.

5. Using the **Window Layout Properties** dialogue box as shown in Figure 5.9 we can also alter the way that the **Preview Pane** is displayed. By default Outlook Express displays the message body below the e-mail headers but you can display the body alongside the headers by selecting **Beside messages** in the **Preview Pane** section and then clicking on the **Apply** button followed by the **OK** button. Your Outlook Express window should now look like the example shown in Figure 5.12.

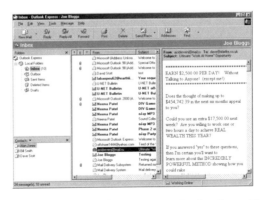

Figure 5.12 Displaying the message body alongside the message headers.

step **6.** Notice that the **Preview Pane** has a grey header block at the top as shown in Figure 5.13. We can remove this by un-checking the **Show preview pane header** tick box in the **Preview Pane** section of the **Window Layout Properties** dialogue box.

Figure 5.13 The Preview Pane header.

step **7.** We can even remove the **Preview Pane** entirely by un-checking the **Show preview pane** tick box in the **Preview Pane** section of the **Window Layout Properties** dialogue box. When you click on the **Apply** button followed by the **OK** button your Outlook Express window should look like the example shown in Figure 5.14.

shortcut

> **To view the contents of a mail message when there is no Preview Pane being displayed simply double click on the message header and a new window will open up displaying the full message content.**

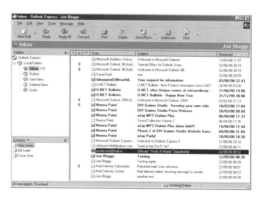

Figure 5.14 Removing the Preview Pane.

8. The standard Toolbar in Outlook Express looks like the example shown in Figure 5.15. However, using the **View I Layout...** option on the Menu Bar we can change this default Toolbar by clicking on the **Customize Toolbar...** button which displays a dialogue box as shown in Figure 5.16.

Figure 5.15 The standard Toolbar in Outlook Express.

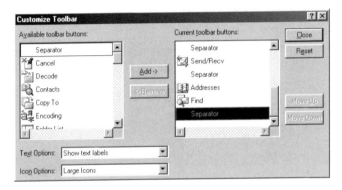

Figure 5.16 Customising the Outlook Express toolbar.

9. Using the **Customize Toolbar** dialogue box you can **Add** or **Remove** toolbar buttons, **Move** toolbar buttons to new positions, and if necessary **Reset** the Toolbar to the default standard layout. When you have finished customising the toolbar click on the **Close** button and then click on the **Apply** button followed by the **OK** button on the **Window Layout Properties** dialogue box.

Summary

In this section we have seen how it is possible to change the display modes within Outlook Express so that different components are visible. You can display or hide the Contacts window, the Folders list and any of the control or information bars. In addition, you can alter the way in which the Preview Pane area displays information. Finally we have learnt how it is possible to modify or customise the standard Toolbar to add or remove the various tool icons available.

Review Questions

1. What is the basic procedure for starting Outlook Express from the Windows desktop?

2. When running Outlook Express for the very first time what must you do before you can send or receive any e-mail messages?

3. What icon is used to signify that a mail message has been read?

4. Which keyboard key should you press to invoke the online Help in Outlook Express?

5. Which Menu Bar option would you use to change the appearance of Outlook Express?

6. How can you stop Outlook Express displaying message header information in the Preview Pane?

7. What procedure would you use to add an icon to the Toolbar?

8. How can you reset the Toolbar to the default configuration?

Messaging

Obviously the most important aspects of using Outlook Express are the procedures for sending and receiving messages to and from other e-mail users. Therefore we will now look at the messaging capabilities of Outlook Express in more detail.

6.1. Send a Message

In this section you will see how to use Outlook Express to:

- Create a new message.
- Insert a mail address in the 'To:' field.
- Insert a title in the 'Subject:' field.
- Add an auto-signature to a message.
- Use the spell checking tool.
- Attach a file to a message.
- Send a message with high/low priority.

Exercise 6.1

step **1.** If it is not already open you should start Outlook Express by either double clicking the icon on the desktop or by clicking on the **Start** button on the **Task Bar** and selecting **Programs I Outlook Express**. After the application has started, click on the **Inbox** folder in the **Folders** list to display its contents.

step **2.** There are two ways to create a new message in Outlook Express, either select **Message I New Message** from the Menu Bar or click on the **New Mail** icon on the standard Toolbar. Whichever method you choose to use, a dialogue box like the one shown in Figure 6.1 will appear.

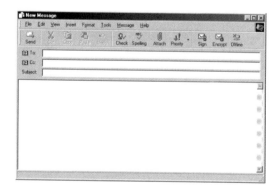

Figure 6.1 Creating a New Message.

3. The first task is to enter the recipient's e-mail address in the **To:** box. This can be any valid e-mail address generally in the format name@somewhere.com, where the first part is the user's name and the second part after the @ sign is their location, as shown in Figure 6.2.

Figure 6.2 Entering an e-mail address.

shortcut

> **If you are using Outlook Express for the very first time you may not have anyone's e-mail address to enter in the To: box. However, you can always send an e-mail message to yourself in order to test the system and see if it is working properly, simply enter your own e-mail address in the To: box.**

4. Next, you should enter a subject or title for the new message in the **Subject:** box. Simply type something relevant concerning the message you are sending as shown in Figure 6.3.

Figure 6.3 Entering a subject or title for a new message.

5. Note that the **Subject:** is optional and you don't have to enter anything in this box if you don't want to. However if you don't type in a **Subject:** you will receive a warning message like the one shown in Figure 6.4 when you try to **Send** the new message.

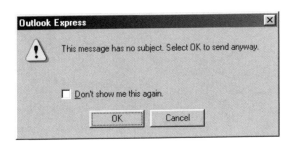

Figure 6.4 Warning message display when a mail message has no Subject.

6. After you have completed the **To:** and **Subject:** boxes you can enter the text of the message in the main area of the **New Message** window, as shown in Figure 6.5. When you have finished typing your message then select **File | Send Message** on the Menu Bar or click on the **Send** icon on the standard Toolbar.

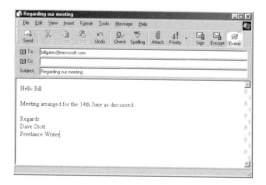

Figure 6.5 The completed new message prior to sending.

7. If you regularly end your new messages with exactly the same words you can setup a Signature using the **Tools | Options... | Signatures** tab from the Menu Bar. This displays a dialogue box as shown in Figure 6.6 and after setting up a Signature you can use the **Insert | Signature** option in the **New Message** window to automatically include the appropriate text at the end of your message body.

Figure 6.6 Creating a signature for automatically signing new messages.

shortcut

Note that if you check the 'Add signatures to all outgoing messages' tick box on the Signatures tab then every time you start a New Message the signature will appear automatically.

8. After you have typed the body of your New Message you can get Outlook Express to check for any spelling mistakes by selecting **Tools | Spelling...** from the New Message Menu Bar or by clicking on the **Spelling** icon on the Toolbar. If any mis-spelt words are found then a dialogue box like the one shown in Figure 6.7 will appear and you can make any corrections.

Figure 6.7 Checking the spelling in a new message.

9. Occasionally you might want to send someone a document or other type of file that you have prepared using another application, such as a spreadsheet. This is known as a file attachment and it allows you to send a file along with a normal mail message. You can do this by selecting **Insert | File Attachment...** from the **New Message** Menu Bar or by clicking on the **Attach** icon on the Toolbar. A dialogue box like the one shown in Figure 6.8 will appear and here you can select a file and click on the **Attach** button to complete the process.

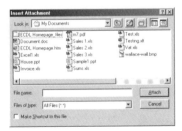

Figure 6.8 Attaching a file to a new message.

10. When you send a new message or reply to a message, you can assign the message a **Priority** so the recipient knows how urgent the message is. There are 3 levels of priority you can set **Low**, **Normal**, and **High**. To set the **Priority** for a new message select **Message | Set Priority** from the **New**

Message Menu Bar or click on the **Priority** icon on the Toolbar and choose the level you require. A new line appears in the **New Message** dialogue box showing the priority if it is set to anything other than normal, as shown in Figure 6.9.

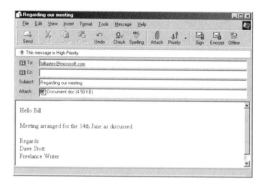

Figure 6.9 A complete message with file attachment and high priority set.

E-mail works by using a system of mailboxes similar to the way that the conventional postal service works. You create your e-mail message on your PC and then post it by sending it to your mail outbox which resides on your ISP's computer. Just like when you post a letter, the delivery of the message takes place automatically once you have posted or sent it. However, there is one important difference between e-mail and the postal service when it comes to receiving messages. With the standard postal service letters are delivered to your address by the postman, you don't normally know that you going to receive anything until it drops through your letterbox. With e-mail however you have to check your incoming mailbox to see if you have received anything and request it to be sent to your computer. This is similar to the situation where you have a P.O. box at the post office and unless you physically go and check its contents you wont know whether you have received anything. Therefore don't just expect new e-mail messages to appear on your PC by magic, instead you should check for incoming e-mail on a regular basis by using the Receive mail options in Outlook Express.

Summary

We have seen in this section that there are several options available when you wish to send an e-mail message. Whilst the address of the recipient is mandatory everything else regarding the message is optional. You can add a Subject, Attach a file, include an automatic Signature, and set the Priority when creating new messages. You can even check the Spelling before you send a message.

6.2. Copy, Move, Delete

When you are creating a new message to send to someone there are a few tools you can use to help you edit the text more easily.

In this section we will look at how to:

● Use Copy and Paste tools to duplicate text within a message or to another active message.
● Use Cut and Paste tools to move text within a message or to another active message.
● Use Cut and Paste tools to insert text from another source into a message.
● Delete text in a message.
● Delete a file attachment from a message.

Exercise 6.2

step **1.** Select **File I New Mail Message** from the Menu Bar or click on the **New Mail** icon to open the **New Message** dialogue box. Enter an address and subject, then type some text in the main body of the message as shown in Figure 6.10.

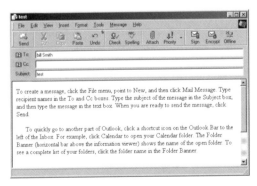

Figure 6.10 Editing text in a message.

step **2.** Select some of the text in the body of the message using the left mouse
button and dragging the pointer across an area of text, the selected text will
be highlighted in black as shown in Figure 6.11. Next, select **Edit | Copy** on
the Menu Bar to copy the selected text into the Clipboard. Position the cursor
somewhere else in the message and now if you select **Edit | Paste** from the
Menu Bar the text which was copied to the Clipboard will be inserted. You
can use the same procedure to copy text from any messages that you have
received into any new messages that you are sending. Similarly, you can use
the Copy and Paste tools along with the Clipboard to copy text from other
applications, such as a word processor, into your messages.

shortcut

**Instead of using the Menu Bar to perform Copy, Cut and
Paste functions via the Clipboard you can click on the
appropriate icons on the Toolbar.**

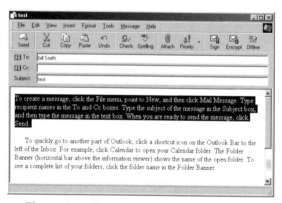

Figure 6.11 Selecting text in a message.

step **3.** To remove text from a message first select it using the mouse and then delete
it using either the Delete key on the keyboard or by using **Edit | Cut** or by
clicking on the **Cut** icon on the Toolbar.

caution!

**The Windows Clipboard only stores one item at a time.
Whenever you use the Edit | Paste function whatever was
last cut or copied to the Clipboard is pasted and this might
not always be what you intended. Therefore you should
consider Cut and Paste or Copy and Paste as a single
function.**

4. If you have attached a file to a new message and then you change your mind and wish to delete the attachment, simply highlight the file name in the **Attach:** box and press the Delete key on the keyboard. The **Attach:** box will then disappear from the **New Message** window.

Summary

Using the Copy, Cut, and Paste tools in conjunction with the Windows Clipboard you can easily edit messages, include text from other applications and delete any text. In addition, you can delete any file attachments if you change your mind about sending them.

6.3. Read a Message

Any e-mail messages that you received will appear in your Inbox and in this section we will learn how to:

● Collect or open mail.
● Mark/highlight a message in a mail folder.
● Use the mail bin.
● Open and save a file attachment.

Exercise 6.3

1. When checking your mail you have 3 options, **Send and Receive**, **Receive** only, or **Send** only. To collect any incoming mail you should select **Tools I Send and Receive I Send and Receive All** or **Receive All** from the Menu Bar or click on the **Send/Recv** icon on the Toolbar.

2. Any new incoming messages will appear in your Inbox. Here you can mark or highlight a message for future attention using the **Message I Flag Message** option on the Toolbar. When you do this a small flag marker appears next to the message header as shown in Figure 6.12.

Figure 6.12 A message 'flagged' in the Inbox.

3. When a message is highlighted, if you press the Delete key on the keyboard then the message will be transferred to the **Deleted Items** folder. This folder acts in the same way as the standard Windows Recycle Bin, and therefore you can recover or undelete messages if you subsequently change your mind. If you wish to completely remove a message from the **Deleted Items** folder then either select in and press the Delete key on your keyboard or click on the **Delete** icon on the toolbar. To remove all the messages from the **Deleted Items** folder, select **Edit | Empty 'Deleted Items' Folder** on the menu bar.

4. To open an attachment you should click on the **Attachment** icon to the right of the message header in the message **Preview Pane** and a drop down menu will appear as shown in Figure 6.13. Simply double click on the attachment you want to open.

Figure 6.13 Opening an attachment.

There are two very important things to consider when dealing with any file attachments that have been sent to you via e-mail. First, in order to open any attachment you must have the appropriate software installed on your PC. This means that if someone sends you for example an Excel spreadsheet you MUST have the Excel application installed on your system to be able to open the file. Second, certain documents and files may contain a virus and these could easily corrupt or delete the data stored on your hard disk. Therefore you should use appropriate Anti-Virus software to check any files that you receive as attachments before opening them, especially if they have come from an unknown source.

5. As well as opening file attachments you can save them in a folder on your hard disk. To do this select the **File | Save Attachments...** option from the Menu Bar or the **Save Attachments...** option on the drop down menu from the **Attachment** icon to the right of the message header in the message **Preview Pane**. A dialogue box like the one shown in Figure 6.14 will appear and you can select any attachments to a message and save them in an appropriate folder.

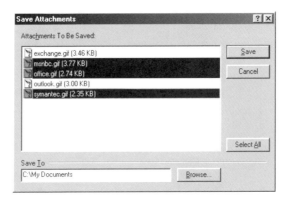

Figure 6.14 Saving attachments.

Summary

In this section we have seen how to collect new mail, open it and view its contents in the Inbox, and how to mark or Flag it for our future attention. Finally, we have looked at how to View and Save any file attachments that we have received.

6.4. Reply to a Message

One of the most common tasks you will be required to perform when using Outlook Express is to reply to messages that you have received.

Therefore, in this section we will look at how to:

● Use reply to sender function.
● Use reply to all function.
● Reply with original message insertion.
● Reply without original message insertion.
● Forward a message.

Exercise 6.4

1. In your Inbox folder select a mail message that you have received by clicking on the message header. To reply to the message select **Message | Reply to Sender** from the Menu Bar or click on the **Reply** icon on the Toolbar. This will display a new message window with the recipient's address and the subject line already filled in preceded by **Re:** to signify that this message is a reply. In addition, the text of the original message will appear in the new message body, as shown in Figure 6.15.

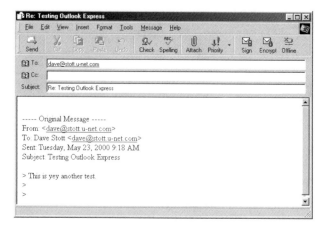

Figure 6.15 Replying to a received message.

2. If a mail message has more than one recipient you can use the **Message I Reply to All** option on the Menu Bar or click on the **Reply All** icon on the Toolbar to send a reply to all the original recipients of the message. When you do this the individual e-mail addresses are automatically added to the **To:** address box in the new message, as shown in Figure 6.16. Notice also that **Re:** has been inserted in front of the subject to indicate that this is a reply to an original message.

Figure 6.16 Replying to all original recipients of a message.

3. Note that by default Outlook Express will include the text from the original message in your replies. You can of course delete this text if you wish. However if you don't want it to be included automatically in the first place you can select **Tools I Options...** from the Menu Bar and then on the **Send** tab uncheck the tick box next to **Include message in reply** option, as shown in Figure 6.17, and then click on the **Apply** button followed by the **OK** button. Now, whenever you reply to a message, none of the original text will be automatically inserted.

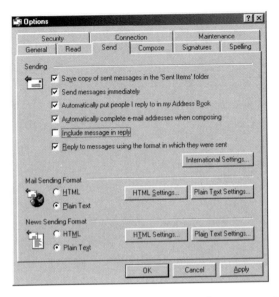

Figure 6.17 Preventing the original text from appearing in replies.

4. As well as replying to a message you have received you can Forward a copy of it to someone else. To do this, select the message you want to forward and then select **Message I Forward** on the Menu Bar or click on the **Forward** icon on the Toolbar. This procedure works in a similar way to replying to a message. However when you forward a message you need to specify a recipient in the **To:** address box as shown in Figure 6.18. Notice also that **Fw:** has been inserted before the subject to indicate that this is a forwarded message.

Figure 6.18 Forwarding a message.

Summary

Replying both to individuals and multiple original recipients of a message is quick and easy in Outlook Express. However, remember that by default the text from the original message will be inserted in your replies but you can turn off this option if you wish. As well as replying you can also forward messages if you want.

Review Questions

1. Which Toolbar icon would you click on to create a new mail message?

2. What symbol is used to separate the 2 parts of an e-mail address?

3. What happens if you don't include a Subject line in a new mail message?

4. How can you automatically sign each new mail message that you create?

5. Which Menu Bar option would you use to check the spelling in a mail message you have created?

6. Which Menu Bar option would you use to attach a file to a mail message?

7. How many priority levels are there for sending mail messages?

8. Why should you check your e-mail post box on a regular basis?

9. How many items can be stored in the Windows Clipboard at any one time?

10. How can you remove an attached file from a mail message?

11. What is the procedure for viewing attachments?

12. Which Toolbar icon would you click on to reply to everyone that was sent a mail message?

13. How can you prevent the original text from a mail message from appearing in your replies?

14. What is the difference between Forward and Reply?

Addressing

In this chapter you will learn how to

- *Add a mail address to an address list*
- *Update an address book from incoming mail*
- *Delete a mail address from an address list*
- *Create a new address/distribution list*
- *Replying to a message using a distribution list*
- *Copy a message to another address*
- *Use the Carbon copy and Blind copy options*

As you start to use Outlook Express regularly you will probably send and receive mail messages from a number of different people and each time you create a new message you will have to enter a suitable e-mail address (unless you are replying to one that you have received). Fortunately, Outlook Express has an Address Book where you can record all sorts of details about the people you are in regular contact with. Most importantly it allows you to record e-mail addresses for future use.

7.1. Using Address Books

In this section we will cover the basic features of the Outlook Express Address Book and in particular how to:

● Add a mail address to an address list.
● Update an address book from incoming mail.
● Delete a mail address from an address list.
● Create a new address list/distribution list.

Exercise 7.1

step **1.** There are two ways you can add a mail address to the Address Book. If you have received a mail message from someone, you can select the message by clicking on the message header and then select **Tools I Add Sender to Address Book** on the Menu Bar. The new address will then appear in the **Contacts** window if it is currently displayed, as shown in Figure 7.1. Alternatively you can select **Tools I Address Book...** on the Menu Bar or click on the **Addresses** icon on the Toolbar, which displays a new dialogue box as shown in Figure 7.2.

Figure 7.1 The Contacts window.

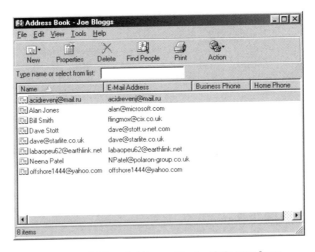

Figure 7.2 The Address Book dialogue box.

2. In the **Address Book** dialogue box you should select **File I New Contact...** to add someone's e-mail address and a tabbed dialogue **Properties** windows will appear as shown in Figure 7.3. Here you can simply fill in the required boxes, click on the **Add** button and then the **OK** button when you have finished. Notice that there are several other tabs on this window which allow to you record comprehensive details about a particular contact if you so wish.

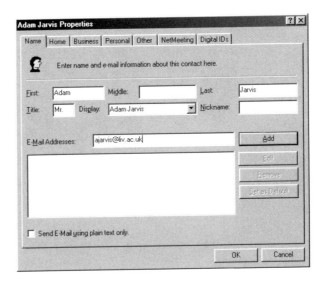

Figure 7.3 Adding a new contact to the Address Book.

shortcut

> **By default there is an option on the Send tab under Tools |**
> **Options.. which will automatically put people that you**
> **reply to in the address book. However you can turn this**
> **option off if you wish.**

3. You can delete a contact either by selecting it in the **Contacts** window or
the **Address Book** and then pressing the **Delete** key on your keyboard, or
selecting **File | Delete** on the Menu Bar, or by clicking on the **Delete** icon
on the Toolbar. Whichever method you choose a warning message will appear
asking you to confirm the deletion process as shown in the example in Figure
7.4.

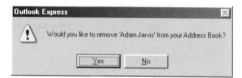

Figure 7.4 Delete Contact confirmation.

4. There may be occasions when you want to send the same mail message to a
number of people at the same time. You can do this by typing multiple e-mail
addresses in to the **To:** box when creating a new message, separating each
one by a semi-colon or a comma. However, there is a better way if this is
something that you want to do on a regular basis, which involves setting up a
distribution list. To do this open up the Address Book and select **File | New**
Group... from the Menu Bar. This displays a new dialogue box and you
should enter an appropriate name for your new group in the **Group Name:**
box as shown in Figure 7.5.

Figure 7.5 Creating a new group.

5. Next, click on the **Select Members** button and another dialogue box appears where you can choose which of your current contacts should be members of the Group as shown in Figure 7.6. Once you are satisfied with the make up of your Group click on the **OK** button and then on the **OK** button again on the previous group **Properties** dialogue box.

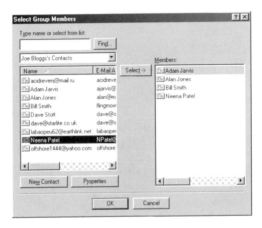

Figure 7.6 Selecting contacts to become group members.

6. Your Address Book should now look like the example shown in Figure 7.7. If you now select **View | Folders and Groups** from the Address Book Menu Bar you will see a list of folders and groups displayed on the left hand side of the window. Clicking on a Group name displays a list of the group members as shown in Figure 7.8.

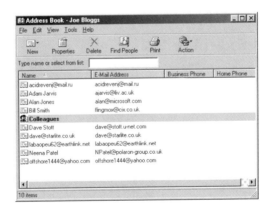

Figure 7.7 A Group in the Address Book.

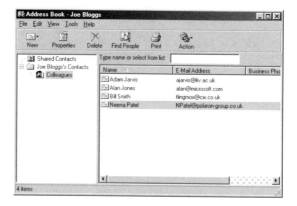

Figure 7.8 Displaying a list of Group Members.

Summary

By using the Address Book features in Outlook Express you can maintain a list of regular contacts so that you don't have to keep typing in their e-mail addresses when you want to send them a message. You can add contacts to the Address Book in various ways and set up Groups with specific members that you can use as a distribution list.

7.2. Messages to Several Addresses

In this section we will look at how we can:

● Reply to a message using a distribution list.
● Copy a message to another address.
● Use the blind copy option.

Exercise 7.2

1. We have already seen how we can send a message to multiple recipients by adding their e-mail addresses to the **To:** box but if you have a Group set up in your Address Book you can simply select the Group name as the **To:** entry, as shown in Figure 7.9. The result will be that all the Group members will receive the message.

Figure 7.9 Sending mail to a Group.

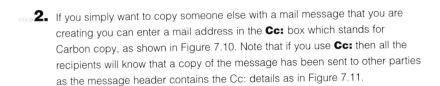
2. If you simply want to copy someone else with a mail message that you are creating you can enter a mail address in the **Cc:** box which stands for Carbon copy, as shown in Figure 7.10. Note that if you use **Cc:** then all the recipients will know that a copy of the message has been sent to other parties as the message header contains the Cc: details as in Figure 7.11.

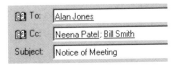

Figure 7.10 Using Cc: to send a copy of a message to other recipients.

Figure 7.11 The message header shows that a Cc: has been sent to another party.

3. There is a way of sending a copy of a message to other recipients so that they are unaware of anyone else receiving the message and that is to use what is known as a Blind carbon copy. To do this when you are selecting recipient click on the **Bcc: ->** button instead of the **Cc: ->** button, as shown in Figure 7.12 and a Blind carbon copy will be sent.

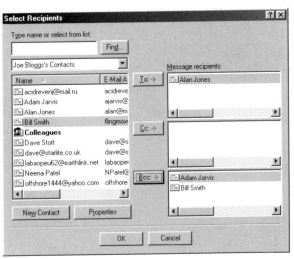

Figure 7.12 Sending Blind carbon copies of a message.

Summary

In this section we have seen how by using a Group defined in the Address Book we can send a message to any number of recipients all at once. In addition, using Cc: we can send a Carbon copy of a message to someone else but if we want to preserve confidentiality we might need to use Bcc: to send Blind carbon copies instead.

Review Questions

1. You have received a mail message from someone that you have not communicated with before. How can you add their e-mail address to your list of Contacts?

2. What is the procedure for deleting a Contact from your Address Book?

3. How can you send the same mail message to a large group of people?

4. What is the principle difference between Cc: and Bcc:?

Message Management

In this chapter you will learn how to

- *Search for a message*
- *Create a new mail folder*
- *Delete a message*
- *Move messages to a new mail folder*
- *Sort messages by criteria such as name, subject and date*

As time goes by you will probably accumulate a significant number of mail messages and you will need to organise and manage them for easy reference.

8.1. Organising Messages

In the final section of this guide we will learn how to:

● Search for a message.
● Create a new mail folder.
● Delete a message.
● Move messages to a new mail folder.
● Sort messages by name, by subject, by date etc.

Exercise 8.1

step **1.** When you have accumulated a large number of messages in your Inbox you might find it difficult to locate a specific message that you received a long time ago. In this case you can use the **Edit I Find I Message...** option on the Menu Bar or click on the **Find** icon on the Toolbar. This displays a dialogue box like the one shown in Figure 8.1 and here you can enter various details about the message you are trying to locate. Obviously the more specific the detail you enter in the various boxes the more likely you are to find precisely the message(s) that you are looking for, so enter as many details as you can.

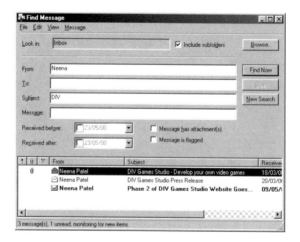

Figure 8.1 Using Find to locate specific messages.

step **2.** Whilst by default all incoming messages end up in your Inbox, you can if you wish create other Folders in which to store various messages. To create a new

folder select **File I Folder I New** from the Menu Bar and you will see a dialogue box like the example in Figure 8.2. Note that new folders are created within the existing hierarchical folder tree structure so in our example the folder **Work related messages** will be created as a sub-folder of **Old mail Messages** as shown in the subsequent Folders window illustrated in Figure 8.3.

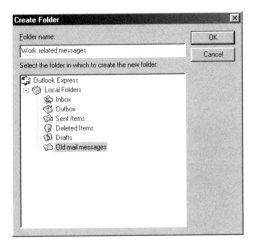

Figure 8.2 Creating a new folder to store messages in.

Figure 8.3 The new folders structure.

3. Once you have created some new folders to store your messages in, you will probably need to move some messages from their existing folders. To do this select the message you want to move by clicking on the message header and then select **Edit I Move to Folder...** on the Menu Bar. A dialogue box like the one shown in Figure 8.4 will appear and here you can select a target

89

folder for the message to be moved to. Note you can also use the **File |
Copy to Folder...** option on the Menu Bar and this will leave the original
message intact whilst making a copy of it in the target folder.

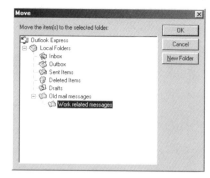

Figure 8.4 Moving a message to another folder.

shortcut

**When selecting a message to move or copy to another
folder, if you hold down the Ctrl key on the keyboard you
can select multiple messages at the same time. You can
also move messages between folders quickly and easily by
selecting them and dragging them to a new location using
the mouse.**

4. To remove an entire message from the Inbox or any other folder simply select
the message header and press the Delete key on your keyboard or click on
the **Delete** icon on the Toolbar. This procedure doesn't actually delete the
message immediately but instead it moves the message to the **Deleted
Items** folder, as shown in Figure 8.5, where you either delete it completely or
move it to another folder if you wish. You can also clear the entire contents of
the **Deleted Items** folder by selecting **Edit | Empty 'Deleted Items'
Folder** from the Menu Bar.

Figure 8.5 The Deleted Items folder.

5. Finally when organising messages within folders you can use the **View** |
Sort by... option on the Menu Bar to automatically sort messages into a
specific order. For example, you can sort by **Priority**, **Attachment**, **Flag**,
From (sender), **Subject** or **Received date** in either ascending or
descending order. The example in Figure 8.6 shows the Inbox with all the
messages sorted in ascending order of the From field.

Figure 8.6 Sorting messages within folders.

shortcut

> To sort messages in a folder quickly and easily you can
> click on the individual column headings and the messages
> will be sorted based on that column. Clicking on the same
> column heading a second time reverses the sort order.

Summary

In this chapter we have seen that Outlook Express provides several
different tools and features to help us organise and manage our
messages. We can create new folders, move and copy messages
between folders, delete messages and sort them into various ascending
or descending orders.

Review Questions

1. Which Toolbar icon would you click on to find a specific message
in a folder?

2. What is a sub-folder and how can you create one?

3. Which Menu Bar option would you use to copy a message to a
particular folder?

4. Which keyboard key should you hold down to select multiple
messages in a folder?

5. What happens when you delete a mail message in your Inbox?

6. Which Menu Bar option would you use to sort the messages in a folder so that they appear in chronological order?

Final Summary

Now that you have reached the end of this guide you should have gained a good insight into the principles of using Internet Explorer to browse the Web, Outlook Express to communicate via e-mail and, most importantly, a basic appreciation of the Internet itself. However, this guide is not intended to be a fully comprehensive training manual for Internet Explorer or Outlook Express and there are many aspects of these two packages which have not been covered. In addition there are a myriad of other aspects of using the Internet in general. Therefore, you are encouraged to further explore the capabilities and features of both Internet Explorer and Outlook Express in order to broaden your knowledge of these software packages.

The Internet is so large and contains such a vast amount of information (some good, some not so good) on all sorts of subjects that it really is an invaluable resource and research tool. As you start to explore it and find more and more interesting things it can become addictive. However, one thing is certain, the Internet has become so important on a global scale that it is impossible to ignore!

Index

European Computer Driving Licence™

the european pc skills standard

Springer's study guides have been designed to complement the ECDL syllabus, and be consistent with the content contained within it. Each study guide enables you to successfully complete the European Driving Licence (ECDL). The books cover a range of specific knowledge areas and skill sets, with clearly defined learning objectives, broken down into seven modules.

Each module has been written in clear, jargon-free language, with self-paced exercises and regular review questions, to help prepare you for ECDL Tests.

Titles in the series include:

- **Module 1: Basic Concepts of Information Technology**
  ISBN: 1-85233-442-8   Softcover   £9.95

- **Module 2: Using the Computer & Managing Files**
  ISBN: 1-85233-443-6   Softcover   £9.95

- **Module 3: Word Processing**
  ISBN: 1-85233-444-4   Softcover   £9.95

- **Module 4: Spreadsheets**
  ISBN: 1-85233-445-2   Softcover   £9.95

- **Module 5: Database**
  ISBN: 1-85233-446-0   Softcover   £9.95

- **Module 6: Presentation**
  ISBN: 1-85233-447-9   Softcover   £9.95

- **Module 7: Information & Communication**
  ISBN: 1-85233-448-7   Softcover   £9.95

All books are available, of course, from all good booksellers (who can order them even if they are not in stock), but if you have difficulties you can contact the publisher direct by telephoning +44 (0) 1483 418822 or by emailing orders@svl.co.uk

For details of other Springer books and journals, please visit

www.springer.de

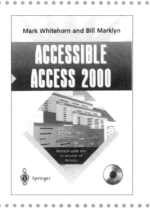